RURAL REALITIES

HEMANT SINGH

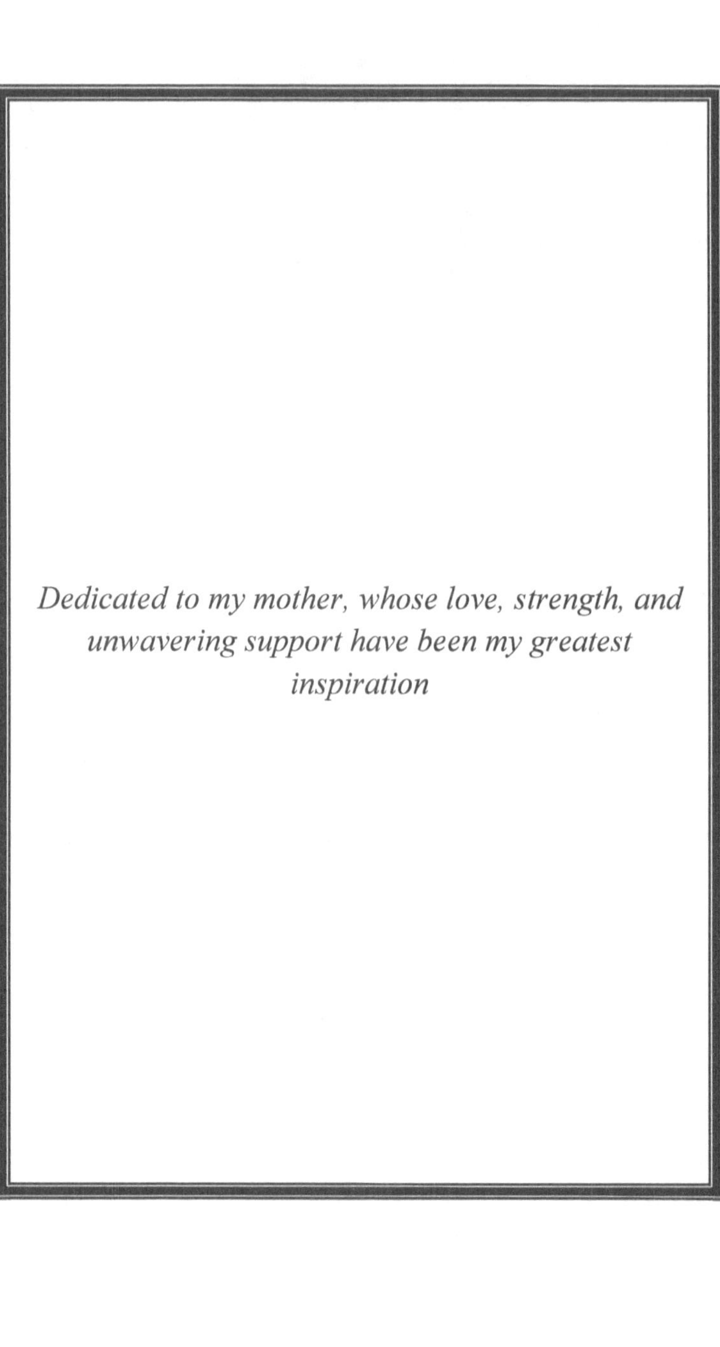

Dedicated to my mother, whose love, strength, and unwavering support have been my greatest inspiration

This page is intentionally left blank

About the author

Hemant is an analyst by profession, entrepreneur by choice, and advocate for sustainable innovation at heart. Passionate about environmental responsibility and rural development, he has worked on initiatives that transform agricultural waste into opportunity- manufacturing paper from peels, utilizing cow dung for eco-friendly applications, transforming eggshells into nutrient-rich manure, and promoting sustainable farming methods like hydroponics and aquaponics. He also aims to empower local and underserved communities by creating opportunities through sustainable solutions. His debut book, Rural Realities, is a deep exploration of socio-economic challenges in rural India, offering first-hand insights from the people at the heart of these issues. With a vision to bridge entrepreneurship and grassroots action, he continues to explore sustainable solutions that drive meaningful change.

Table of Contents

Acknowledgement

Exploring 'Rural Realities' and encapsulating its essence as a memoir in this book, has been a transformative journey, one that would not have been possible without the unwavering support of some of my dearest people.

First and foremost, I want to thank my family for their encouragement, understanding, and endless patience as I travelled across villages, spent late nights writing, and pursued this project with all my heart. Your love and belief in me have been my anchor.

To Srishti, my precious, who stood by me at every step of the way - your love, support, and occasional dose of encouragement has given me the strength I needed to see this project through. Thank you for always believing in me, even when I doubted myself.

Finally, I can't go without making a mention of all the people whom I met at each village - thank you for opening up about your lives to me and for sharing your stories, struggles, and dreams. This book is for you and because of you. Your voices and experiences are the soul of Rural Realities, and I am deeply grateful to have had the privilege to witness it up close.

Thank you all for being part of this journey.

Introduction

Rural Realities is a journey into the heart of North India - a world often depicted in broad strokes but rarely seen up close. This book emerged from my travels across villages in Uttar Pradesh, Rajasthan, Haryana, Uttarakhand, and Punjab, where, over the course of 15 months, I engaged with residents who shared with me their lives, challenges, and hopes. Each chapter is dedicated to one of these 21st century backwaters, highlighting a specific issue that shapes the daily experiences of those who live there.

From the excruciating impact of poverty and caste discrimination to the catastrophic environmental degradation and strained resources at pilgrimage sites, I encountered these issues not merely through distant observations but via extensive in-person engagement and meaningful conversations with the people affected. In Mathura, Tehsil Sikrai, Ayodhya, Etawah, Haridwar, and numerous other villages, I heard their stories, which revealed to me, a spirit of interminable resilience contemporaneously underscoring their daily struggles, often overlooked in urban narratives.

This book does not aim to point fingers at any governing bodies or institutions. Rather, it is my hope that Rural Realities serves as a mirror, encouraging readers to visualize these challenges with consideration, as fellow human experiences, not statistics. Each chapter invites curiosity and reflection on what these realities mean for us all, perhaps inspiring readers to find ways, however small, to make a difference.

Through Rural Realities, my intention is to offer a glimpse into the lives of those who make up the fabric of rural India. My hope is that this book inspires empathy and a sense of shared responsibility, encouraging all of us to take personal steps to support communities in need, bridging the gap between awareness and action.

The Never-Well

In march 2023, during my visit to a village near Mathura, called Kashi Purwa, I immediately noticed something unsettling. As I walked through the narrow lanes, I saw multiple adults and even children with visible body deformities - swollen joints, crooked limbs, and bowed legs. It wasn't just a rare occurrence; many of the people I encountered seemed to be affected. The atmosphere was calm, but the sight of so many suffering in silence weighed heavily on me.

Curious and concerned, I stopped by a small tea stall and started a conversation with a man in his early 30s named Mriduk, who was sitting nearby. He appeared healthy, but there was an air of quiet resignation about him, as if he had grown accustomed to the hardships surrounding him.

"Why are there so many people here with such deformities? Is this common in your village?" I asked, trying to understand what was happening.

Mriduk stirred his tea thoughtfully before answering. "It's the water. The groundwater here is contaminated with fluoride and other harmful chemicals. We've been drinking this water for years. It affects our bones, our teeth, everything. Children grow up with deformities, and adults develop all kinds of health problems."

His words were blunt, but the reality was far from simple. The very thing that should sustain life - water was slowly poisoning this village. He pointed to the nearest hand pump, explaining that despite their efforts to bring clean water, most sources were tainted. The contamination was so deeply embedded in the groundwater that it was almost impossible to avoid.

The issue of water contamination has become an alarming public health crisis, affecting countless communities around the world. Polluted water sources, whether from industrial waste, agricultural runoff, or untreated sewage, are now common in many areas, leading to severe health consequences for those who rely on these waters for drinking, cooking, and bathing. Contaminants such as heavy metals, pesticides, and toxic chemicals seep into rivers, lakes, and groundwater, spreading invisible yet potent hazards. This exposure causes numerous health problems, including respiratory diseases, gastrointestinal disorders, and long-term ailments like cancer.

One of the gravest impacts of water contamination is the occurrence of severe, sometimes life-threatening health conditions. High levels of chemicals like lead, arsenic, and mercury are associated with serious illnesses, such as cancers, organ damage, and, in severe cases, physical deformities. For instance, communities that depend on groundwater contaminated with arsenic or fluoride are at high risk for conditions like skeletal fluorosis, which causes bone deformities and chronic pain. Additionally, water tainted with industrial pollutants has been linked to birth defects, developmental delays in children, and reproductive health problems, with long-term effects that extend through generations.

The effects of contaminated water are not only devastating to individuals but also weaken entire communities. When people are forced to endure chronic illness and spend limited resources on medical treatment, their ability to work and contribute to society is severely impaired. Children, especially, bear the consequences, as they may be too sick to attend school or, in extreme cases, are born with conditions that limit their physical and mental potential. Families burdened by healthcare costs and lack of clean water sources find it harder to break free from poverty, perpetuating cycles of disadvantage and reduced opportunity.

The consequences of polluted water reach far beyond personal health, impacting agricultural productivity and food safety as well. Crops irrigated with contaminated water absorb harmful chemicals, introducing toxins into the food supply and endangering the health of consumers. Livestock are similarly affected when they drink polluted water, leading to further risks as toxins enter the food chain. These effects on food safety make it clear that water contamination is not just an isolated problem - it is a crisis that affects every facet of life.

I listened as he continued, "We know the water is bad, but what choice do we have? The government installed some filtration systems years ago, but they stopped working. No one came back to repair them, and the people here can't afford to buy bottled water or install new filters."

The issue wasn't just neglect; it was a vicious cycle of poverty and lack of resources. Without access to clean water, the people of Kashi Purwa had no choice but to rely on contaminated sources. Over time, this led to the widespread physical deformities some of which I had seen, along with other health problems like stomach issues, joint pain, and even organ damage.

"Have any efforts been made recently to solve this?" I asked, wondering if any progress had been made.

"Not really," Mriduk said, shaking his head. "There have been a few visits from NGOs, and we've had politicians make promises during election season. But once the elections are over, we're forgotten again. The problem isn't new, We've been dealing with it for as long as I can remember."

His words echoed the larger reality of rural India, where many villages face similar challenges but lack the necessary infrastructure and support to address them. It wasn't just a case study, limited to Kashi Purwa.

When I looked into the situation further, I learned that other villages, like Gangnauli in Uttar Pradesh aka the 'cancer district' of Uttar Pradesh, were also grappling with water contamination. In Gangnauli, contaminated water from river Krishna which happens to be third largest river by volume had led to severe skin problems, cancers, and cognitive impairments. Despite efforts to install water treatment plants, they too had fallen into disrepair, leaving the villagers to fend for themselves.

Back in Mathura, the people of Kashi Purwa continued to suffer. Mriduk, like many others, knew that the situation wasn't going to change overnight. "We're not asking for much," he said, his voice steady but tired. "We just want clean water, something safe to drink. We've seen too many people get sick, too many children grow up with these deformities. This shouldn't be our reality."

His words stuck with me. Water, the most basic necessity of life, was out of reach for so many in these villages. And yet, the issue of contaminated water remained largely unnoticed, hidden beneath the grandeur of cities like Mathura and the slow-moving wheels of bureaucracy.

Addressing the issue of water contamination requires a collective commitment to stricter regulations, sustainable waste management, and investment in clean water infrastructure. Without urgent action, communities will continue to suffer the devastating consequences of unsafe water, with effects rippling outwards, touching health, economy, and social stability. Recognizing this issue and encouraging conversation about the realities of water contamination is a critical first step in mobilizing efforts toward safer, cleaner water for all.

Mathura, a city of immense religious and cultural significance, is known worldwide as the birthplace of Lord Krishna. Every year, thousands of pilgrims visit the temples, ghats, and sacred sites, bathing in the holy Yamuna River and soaking in the spiritual atmosphere. However, beneath the layers of devotion and history lies a problem often overlooked- the severe issue of water contamination in the rural areas surrounding this ancient city.

The question we must all ask ourselves is this: **How can we, as a society, continue to allow villages like Kashi Purwa and Gangnauli to suffer from something as fundamental as lack of clean drinking water?**

In a world where technological advancements are made daily, why is it so difficult to provide safe water to our most vulnerable populations? This isn't just an environmental issue; but a matter of fundamental human rights. The time for deliberations is long gone, now it's time for initiative and action, before more lives are affected.

Remember, we as a nation are answerable to Mriduk.

The crumbling Earth

In may 2023, I was at Etawah, Uttar Pradesh, assisting my father for his construction related work. It was late so i wanted to rush back to home as soon as possible, completing this tedious 3 hour drive. As I prepared to head home, turned on the engine, drove a few miles. Out of the blue, I heard a loud thud that interrupted my smooth and hasty swift ride - I had a puncture. I had recently undergone a knee surgery, so changing the tire myself wasn't an option. I started my midnight search for an open and functional puncture shop.

I had almost lost all hope, when I spotted a feeble figure of a person walking by. Had it been a megacity, he would've surely passed without any consideration. However, the beauty and simplicity of rural India is such, that even at that grim hour, he stopped to ask and offer help. Upon inquiring, he told me that there was a puncture shop just around the corner, so with a deep sigh of relief, I rushed to that place and saw a small, flickering light coming from the crooked entrance of a thatched brick-hut in the distance. Panting, I finally reached the shop, where the owner was at the verge brink of closing down and winding up for the day. A middle-aged man named Ajmal greeted me with a tired hello. I explained my situation, so he told me to drive the car to his shop slowly so that he could fix the tire with the help of an electric jack.

When I returned to my car, I noticed that it was unlocked (I skipped a heartbeat) but thankfully nothing was stolen. I drove it back to his shop. He immediately started to get the job done; he might have been in a hurry as well. I noticed that his hands were stained with grease as he began to assess my tire.

"You're lucky it's just a puncture," he said, removing the tire. "You could've had a blowout."

"Yeah, I guess I should be grateful," I replied.

While I was sitting there, with no other means of passing my next few minutes, I started to look around. Though it was dark, but I could notice that outside there was vast empty land with no buildings, structures or even crops.\

"Is this your land?" I asked, looking around at the dry patches of earth near the shop.

"Yes," he replied with a tint of sadness in his voice.

"Why don't you farm it, it will give you better earnings than this puncture shop or maybe you can do both and have multiple sources of income." I asked.

"We can't do so." he replied, rather promptly. It seemed as if he was used to this question. I, too, asked for the reason immediately.

Ajmal paused, glancing up. "It's the brick kilns. They have ruined the land."

"Really? How so?" I asked.

"My family has owned this land for generations," he began. "We used to grow crops - wheat, sugarcane, things that fed us. But later my grandfather gave this land to a brick kiln contractor,"

"So, I can't farm it anymore." "Why not?" I pressed.

"Because it's unfertile now," Ajmal said, shaking his head. "The demand for bricks exploded. Builders want them for everything. So the kilns spread everywhere, stripping the land of resources. The air is filled with smoke, and it settles on everything. You can't even breathe properly sometimes."

The proliferation of brick kilns and similar industrial activities pose a significant threat to soil fertility, particularly in regions heavily reliant on agriculture. These kilns, often found in developing countries, consume vast quantities of clay, soil, and biomass, leading to the degradation of land that has been cultivated for generations. The extraction of soil for brick making not only disrupts the natural ecosystem but also leaves behind barren, infertile landscapes that are unable to support crop growth.

As the demand for bricks escalates, especially in urban areas where rapid construction is underway, the surrounding agricultural land is increasingly sacrificed for industrial expansion. The clay that is extracted from the earth is not merely a resource; it represents a critical layer of the soil that contains essential nutrients and microorganisms necessary for healthy plant growth. When this topsoil is stripped away, it leads to a significant decline in soil health, affecting its structure, fertility, and overall capacity to retain water. Without this vital layer, the soil becomes compacted, dry, and unable to support agricultural productivity.

The consequences of this degradation extend beyond barren fields. Farmers who once relied on their land for sustenance find themselves facing declining yields and increased uncertainty. As the fertility of the soil diminishes, crops become less resilient to pests and diseases, leading to further losses. The inability to produce sufficient food can drive farmers into poverty, forcing them to seek employment in urban areas or turn to less sustainable forms of agriculture that can further deplete the soil. This cycle of degradation not only affects individual livelihoods but also threatens food security for entire communities.

Moreover, the environmental impact of brick kilns is compounded by their emissions, which contribute to air pollution and climate change. The burning of fossil fuels and biomass in these kilns releases greenhouse gases and particulate matter, further destabilizing the delicate balance of local ecosystems. As air quality deteriorates, the health of nearby residents suffers, leading to respiratory illnesses and other health issues that place additional burdens on healthcare systems.

In many cases, the economic incentives driving the growth of brick kilns overshadow the environmental and social costs associated with their operations. Local governments, often under pressure to support industrial growth, may overlook the long-term consequences of soil depletion and environmental degradation. Communities that depend on agriculture for their livelihoods find themselves caught in a web of exploitation and neglect, where their voices are silenced, and their needs go unaddressed

Additionally, the loss of fertile land due to brick kilns can lead to social unrest and conflicts over resources. As agricultural land diminishes, competition for the remaining fertile plots can escalate, creating tensions between farmers and industrial operators. This dynamic can foster an environment of mistrust and hostility, further fracturing community bonds.

"Doesn't the government do anything?" I asked, hoping for some sign of support for people like him.

"They've started to apply some regulations, but it's too late for us. The damage is done. Fertility doesn't just come back. It's like we've broken a bond with nature, and we're paying for it. Look at my land," he said, gesturing around him. "It's all I have, and it's useless."

"Have you tried different crops?" I suggested, wanting to help.

Ajmal let out a bitter laugh. "We've tried everything. But when the soil is tainted, it doesn't matter what you plant. It just won't grow. Even the water is getting scarce. The kilns use so much for their operations that the villagers barely have enough left for themselves."

As I listened to him, I felt the weight of his despair "Do you think there's hope for change?" I asked.

Ajmal looked at me, a mix of resignation and determination in his eyes. "Hope is all we have. But hope without action is just a dream. We need better practices, sustainable alternatives. Otherwise, our children will inherit a wasteland."

As I drove away that night, Ajmal's words stayed with me: **What will it take for us to realize that our actions today are shaping the world of tomorrow?**

In the face of such clear evidence of environmental degradation, I found myself asking: Are we willing to confront the consequences of our choices, or will we continue to prioritize immediate gains over the long-term health of our planet?

The empty fields that used to be full of life reminded me of the lasting harm we can do to nature. The pollution from the brick kilns, which seems necessary for economic growth, has darkened the whole area. It hit me hard that our quest for progress has come with a heavy price. I kept asking myself whether we are really willing to face the fallout from our actions or if we'll just keep ignoring the problem, hoping it will go away on its own.

Pilgrimage plunder

The sun hung low over the hills, casting a golden glow over the valley. The distant hum of temple bells from Haridwar blended with the chirping of birds, creating an oddly peaceful contrast to the concerns weighing on Ramesh's mind. He sat under the shade of an ancient peepal tree, his weathered hands resting on his knees, eyes fixed on the river winding through the plains below.

"Pilgrims come in the millions now," Ramesh began, his voice tinged with both awe and resignation. "And while it brings life to the temples and markets, it drains the villages and rivers."

The influx of people, drawn by faith and tradition, had turned Haridwar into a bustling pilgrimage hub. What had once been a serene place of worship had now become a crowded, resource strained city struggling under the weight of its visitors.

"How so?" I asked, eager to understand his perspective.

Ramesh leaned forward. "Take the Ganga, for example. Everyone comes to take a dip, believing it purifies their soul. But what purifies the Ganga?" He chuckled bitterly. "The garbage left behind, the waste, the plastic - no one thinks of that. The river is burdened, and now the villages upstream, like ours, feel the impact too."

For centuries, the Ganga had been revered as a goddess, a divine force that cleansed sins and sustained life. But faith alone could not protect it from pollution. The once, crystal, waters now carried plastic waste, untreated sewage, and remnants of ritual offerings, turning sacredness into neglect.

I glanced at the dry patches in the surrounding fields. "Are the water sources drying up?"

Ramesh nodded gravely. "Yes, it's become a real problem. When the pilgrims come, water is diverted to accommodate the hotels, guesthouses, and public baths in Haridwar. It leaves very little for the villages. And it's not just the water-the roads are overrun, the forests cut down to make space for new parking lots and commercial spaces."

The economic boost brought by mass tourism was undeniable, but it came at a heavy cost. Development surged, yet infrastructure remained fragile. Forests that had once provided sustenance and shade were now cleared to accommodate convenience. The land was changing, and not for the better.

Ramesh gestured toward the distant hills. "Just ten years ago, that forest was dense. Wild boars and deer roamed freely, and the streams ran year round. Now, the trees are cut down to make room for more tourists. Do you know how much land was cleared for parking lots for Kumbh Mela alone? Entire stretches of forest. What's left for us? Our wells are running dry, and we're losing the very essence of the place we once called home."

His frustration was palpable. The traditional harmony between man and nature was disintegrating under the pressure of unchecked tourism. Haridwar was not just a city of temples and rituals; it was an ecosystem, a community, and a cultural heritage that risked being lost in the name of modernity.

"What do the authorities do about it?" I asked, hoping there was some intervention.

Ramesh chuckled grimly. "Authorities? They're more focused on managing the crowds. They construct more roads, bridges, and bring in additional facilities for the pilgrims. It boosts the economy temporarily, but they fail to see or perhaps they don't care-that in the long term, they're destroying the very land that people come here to revere."

Tourism, when unchecked, had a paradoxical effect. It preserved cultural and religious traditions while simultaneously eroding the very elements that made them meaningful. The commercialization of faith threatened to strip away authenticity, reducing deep-seated beliefs to transactions and rituals to fleeting experiences.

"The irony is painful," I replied. "People come here to cleanse their souls in the Ganga, yet they're polluting the very river they revere."

"Exactly!" Ramesh exclaimed. "Just look at how much plastic waste is left behind after every festival. People come with faith, but they leave behind filth. And it's not just plastic. People defecate along the riverbanks, and the untreated sewage from the hotels flows right into the Ganga. How can we call it holy when we treat it this way?"

His words carried the weight of a truth too often ignored. The sacredness of a place did not come solely from rituals but from respect - a respect that was waning in the face of convenience.

"Have you tried speaking with anyone - local leaders, environmental groups?" I asked.

Ramesh shook his head. "Who listens? The city's priorities are elsewhere. We're just small villages in the hills. No one cares what happens up here as long as the pilgrimage can continue without disruption. And even if they did care, where would they start? The damage is already done. We need a complete shift in thinking, but that doesn't happen overnight."

As the evening deepened, the fading light painted the landscape in soft hues, but there was an undercurrent of loss in the air. I turned to Ramesh, still pondering his words. "What about the future?" I asked softly. "What do you think will happen if things don't change?"

He sighed deeply, his shoulders slumping. "If things continue like this, the Ganga will be just another polluted river, and the forests will disappear. The pilgrims will still come, but the land they come to worship will be hollowed out, lifeless. **We welcome the pilgrims, but at what cost? Who will take care of these lands when the trees are gone, and the water dries up? Who will answer when the Ganga can no longer carry the weight of our neglect?"**

His question lingered long after our conversation ended. As I bid Ramesh farewell, the reality of his words settled deep in my mind. Haridwar was at a crossroads, caught between reverence and recklessness. If steps were not taken to balance faith with responsibility, there might come a time when the river, the forests, and the very soul of the city would be beyond saving.

This was not just the story of one place. It was a reflection of a global dilemma - how to sustain traditions without sacrificing the environment, how to honor the past while securing the future. And if we failed to find the balance, **would there be anything left to worship at all?**

Struggle for stability

On a blistering afternoon in the heart of Chandni Chowk, the bustling marketplace was a frenzy of movement, with vendors shouting their wares and shoppers weaving through the throngs of people. The sun blazed overhead, and the intense heat made the narrow lanes of the bazaar feel suffocating. The air was thick with the scent of spices, fried street food, and the unmistakable undertone of sweat. It was an environment that felt as if it was constantly in motion, yet there was an underlying sense of stagnation for many who walked its streets.

I, too, felt the weight of the heat bearing down on me as I paused at a street corner to take a gulp of water from my bottle. The air felt thick, almost viscous, and my body was drenched with sweat despite the brief moment of stillness. I wiped my brow, trying to shake off the weariness that clung to me like a second skin.

As I stood there, catching my breath, I noticed a man walking towards me. His movements were slow, deliberate, each step seeming to take more energy than the last. His clothes were coated with a layer of dust, his face drawn and parched, as though the day's heat had sapped him of all strength. He carried a trowel in one hand, his knuckles pale from gripping the worn handle too tightly.

He hesitated for a moment before his eyes met mine, and I saw the faintest flicker of vulnerability in them. With a quiet voice that barely rose above the din of the market, he asked, "Sir, could I have some water?"

I didn't hesitate. I handed him my bottle without a second thought. His hand was rough and calloused as he took it, his fingers trembling slightly. He drank deeply, savoring each slow, measured sip, as if the water wasn't just quenching his thirst but offering some small measure of relief from the oppressive heat.

When he finally lowered the bottle, his lips barely parted in a tired smile. He set the trowel down, wiping his face with the back of his hand. It was clear he'd been working under the harsh sun for hours, perhaps even longer.

"You look exhausted," I said, studying his face. There was a layer of dust on his forehead, a fine film that seemed to coat every inch of his skin. "What have you been up to?"

"Just another long day, sir," he replied with a faint, weary smile. "I need to keep working; there's nothing to send back home otherwise."

I watched him carefully. His words hung in the air, heavy with a meaning that went beyond simple exhaustion. It was a tone I had heard before in the voices of people who lived in a cycle of survival- a cycle that seemed to offer no escape, no reprieve.

"Where's home for you?" I asked, curiosity tugging at me.

"A small village in Bihar, near Purnia," he answered, pausing for a moment as if the mention of his home brought a flicker of something softer in his eyes. "I come to Delhi every few months for work. Back home, there's just not enough to get by."

I could hear the weight of his words, the sadness in the quiet spaces between them. It wasn't just a matter of physical hardship; there was an emotional toll, a sacrifice that had become so deeply embedded in his life that it had almost turned into a form of survival.

"That sounds like quite a journey," I said, my voice softening. "How often do you make it to Delhi?"

"Every season, sir," he replied, and there was a hint of resignation in his voice. "I stay for four or five months, then go back for sowing and harvest. My wife and kids are managing, but it's tough. Every time I leave, it feels like I'm leaving a piece of my heart behind."

The way he spoke of his family struck me deeply. His voice, tinged with an aching tenderness, was a stark contrast to the rough edges of the man before me. It was as though every part of him- his soul, his heart, his very being was tethered to his family, yet separated by miles of distance, by seasons of work.

"It must be difficult to leave your family each time," I ventured, feeling the weight of his words settling in the pit of my stomach.

Jugnu let out a heavy sigh, his face creased with the lines of years spent under the sun. "It's harder than I can express. My children barely recognize me now. When I return, it's as if they've grown overnight. My daughter is learning to read, and my son is becoming a young man. Each return feels like I've missed so much of their lives. But what choice do I have? There's no work for us back home."

There was an unmistakable pain in his voice, the kind that comes from a deep, unspoken longing. He wasn't just missing moments; he was missing whole years of his children's lives - years that could never be reclaimed. The very idea of a father coming and going, always an outsider in his own family's world, was enough to make one wonder about the real cost of survival.

I hesitated before asking, "Wouldn't it be simpler to bring your family with you?"

He shook his head slowly, as if the question itself carried the weight of an impossible dream. "Delhi's too costly, sir. If I brought them here, we'd need a larger place, and the rent would take most of my earnings. Here, I share cramped space with other men - no place for a family. At least back home, we have our own small house, some land, and a sense of dignity. In the city, we'd be packed into a single room, living like strangers."

His words painted a vivid picture of the grim realities faced by seasonal migrants. The promise of a better life in the city, a life that many migrants like him sought, often fell short when confronted with the harshness of urban living. The high cost of rent, the lack of space, and the never ending search for stability- these were just a few of the obstacles that made city life seem like an illusion rather than a solution.

"Do others from your village experience this too?" I asked, sensing that his struggles weren't unique to him alone.

"It's the same for every family, sir," Jugnu replied, his eyes dimming slightly as he spoke. "Men leave for cities like Delhi or Mumbai seeking work while the elderly and women remain behind. Our village feels half-empty. It's like we're tearing our families apart just to survive."

There was a deep sadness in his voice now, a sense of loss that wasn't just about physical separation but about the very fabric of family life being torn apart. The migration cycle, driven by the lack of work in rural areas, was not just an economic necessity- it was an emotional burden that left families fractured and communities disrupted.

I felt a pang of empathy for him and the countless others like him who had no choice but to migrate. "Do you encounter any difficulties here, being away from home?" I asked, my voice reflecting a growing sense of concern.

Jugnu rubbed his face, his hand brushing over the dust and grime that had settled on his skin. "It's not easy, sir. People see us as outsiders. Sometimes they treat us poorly, thinking we're here to overcrowd their city. There are times I've been called names or mocked for how we speak. They don't realize we're just trying to work and feed our families."

The quiet sadness in his voice was palpable. It wasn't anger that filled his words but a quiet resignation, as if he had come to accept that he would always be seen as a stranger in a city that wasn't his own.

"That sounds painful," I said, my words feeling insufficient in the face of the suffering he described. "Have you considered staying here permanently, perhaps leaving farming behind?"

"I've thought about it, sir," Jugnu replied, his tone heavy with uncertainty. "But leaving our land feels like losing our roots. Even though it's small, that land is ours. Life in the city is tough, sometimes cruel. People look down on us because we come from villages. In my village, I'm Jugnu ji, a respected figure; here, I'm just another migrant worker. It feels lonely, like I'm an outsider just trying to get by."

His statements deeply impacted me. The sense of belonging and identity tied to one's homeland transcends physical space. Regardless of the challenges faced in urban environments, the inherent connection to one's land, which provides nourishment and a sense of purpose, is an enduring bond that cannot be entirely severed.

"Do you think more job opportunities in your village would stop people from migrating to cities?" I asked, my mind turning over the possibilities.

Jugnu nodded without hesitation, his eyes steady and unwavering. "Absolutely, sir. If there were even a factory or stable work, we wouldn't have to leave. It's hard enough to work far from family, but to face mistreatment as well… that's even tougher. I didn't come here to be disrespected. We have skills, but city folks often overlook our humanity. If there were jobs at home, we'd all stay."

His words echoed the systemic issue that lay at the heart of seasonal migration. It wasn't just about economic survival- it was about dignity, about being seen as more than just a worker, about having a place in society where one could contribute and thrive.

"What about the next generation?" I asked, my voice reflecting a deep concern. "Are you worried they'll face the same struggles?"

He exhaled slowly, his shoulders sagging under the weight of the question. "I hope not. I want my children to go to school, find work close to home, and live without the burden of insults we endure. It hurts that they see me come and go like a stranger. But if things don't change, I fear they'll live the same life, moving from city to city, facing similar challenges."

As I listened to Jugnu, a sense of helplessness washed over me. His concerns for his children were shared by so many others who faced the same fate. The cycle of migration, of displacement, and of survival was an unending loop that seemed impossible to break.

And yet, the solution was clear. **What was needed wasn't just sympathy or fleeting charity- it was a systemic**

change that provided opportunities where they were most needed. Investment in rural infrastructure, the creation of sustainable jobs, and the promotion of entrepreneurship could empower families to remain rooted in their communities rather than being forced to seek work in distant cities.

More than anything, the issue of seasonal migration raised a fundamental question about the dignity of work and the worth of human lives. As we moved forward, the real challenge would be to ensure that families like Jugnu's, families who sacrificed so much for survival, no longer had to choose between their homes and their livelihoods. The time had come to build a future where no one had to leave their family behind in the pursuit of a better life.

And as I walked away from Jugnu, I couldn't shake the question that had formed in my mind: **How can we ensure that people like him are never again seen as outsiders, as strangers, in the very cities that rely on their labor for survival?**

Degrees without direction

The road leading into Solan village twisted and turned through the verdant hills of Uttarakhand, its edges lined with thick pines and stretches of farmland that bore the weight of generations. The village itself, cradled in the valley, seemed almost untouched by time, yet hidden beneath its rustic charm was a crisis that gnawed at its youth- a quiet, relentless erosion of dreams.

Akash, a young man in his late twenties, walked beside me, Hemant Singh, his hands deep in his pockets. There was an ease to his stride, but his face held the quiet burden of unspoken thoughts. The morning air was crisp, carrying the scent of damp earth and fresh harvest.

"You know," Akash began, his voice carrying the weight of something long unspoken, "when we were kids, we believed education would change everything. That if we studied hard, if we did everything right, the world would open up for us." He looked up at the mountains, their peaks draped in mist, as though seeking an answer from them. "But it didn't quite work that way."

I waited for him to continue, sensing his need to share.

"We went to school, some of us even made it to college in nearby towns. We got our degrees. And then?" Akash let out a soft chuckle, though there was little humor in it. "We came back. We waited. And we're still waiting."

The quiet resignation in his voice was something that had become a part of him, like a shadow that never left. It wasn't just his story, it was the story of countless young men and women who had pinned their hopes on education, only to find themselves in a place that offered no space for their knowledge.

Across India, thousands of educated young adults face a harsh reality. The promise of education, once seen as a guarantee of stability, has become an illusion for many. They return home with degrees, with dreams of white-collar jobs, only to find that their villages offer none. The cities, distant and competitive, provide little refuge. The result? A generation caught in limbo, torn between the love for their land and the need for livelihood.

"What do people do when there's no work for what they studied?" I asked gently, sensing the depth of Akash's disillusionment.

Akash shrugged. "Some take up small businesses, but without support, it's tough. A few leave for cities, but they barely make enough to survive. Most stay. We take up whatever work we can - farming, daily labor things that our parents did." His voice softened, tinged with something close to regret. "We weren't supposed to be here, doing this."

His words reflected a silent epidemic: underemployment. Educated youth finding themselves in jobs that required none of the skills they had spent years acquiring. The dignity of labor was not the issue - it was the gnawing realization that their education had led them nowhere. That, despite their degrees, they were no closer to financial stability or societal progress.

"My parents put everything into my education," Akash continued. "I was the first in my family to go to college. They were so proud." He smiled briefly, but it faded just as quickly. "Now, they don't say much. They just… wait. Like me."

I followed his gaze to a small house in the distance, its walls weathered but standing firm. Generations had lived there, each with the hope that the next would have it better. Yet, the cycle remained unbroken.

The absence of work doesn't just affect livelihoods- it corrodes self-worth. The pressure to succeed, to justify years of education, weighs heavily on these young minds. In many cultures, professional success is deeply tied to familial honor, making failure a deeply personal burden.

"Some days," Akash admitted, "it feels like I've let them down."

His words carried the weight of so many others who had walked the same road. Without employment, confidence dwindled. Self-doubt crept in. And for some, desperation led them down dangerous paths- fraud, cybercrime, illicit dealings. Not because they wanted to, but because they saw no other way.

I hesitated before asking, "Has anyone tried to change things? The government, private companies?"

Akash gave a dry laugh. "They talk. Schemes come and go. Some promise jobs, some promise training. But none of them understand the real problem. The industries don't come here, and the jobs that do exist require connections we don't have." He gestured toward the hills. "We don't want factories ruining this land, but we also don't want to keep living like this. It feels like we're being asked to choose between our home and our future."

The problem wasn't just that there were no jobs. It was that the existing system had no place for these youth. The village wasn't resistant to change- it was waiting for the right kind of change. And perhaps, therein lay the answer.

"What if the solution isn't in trying to bring city jobs here, but in building something unique to this place?" I mused. "Eco-tourism? Sustainable industries? Something that uses what you have, rather than replaces it?"

Akash considered it. "Some have tried small businesses, but they struggle without backing. If people had proper training, funding, a real push- it could work. But right now, we're just surviving."

I saw something flicker in Akash's eyes- a cautious hope. It was clear that people like him hadn't given up; they just needed something to believe in.

As we walked back toward the village, the sun rising higher in the sky, the conversation lingered between us.

"So," Akash asked finally, his voice quieter, more introspective, "how do we make it so that staying home doesn't mean giving up?"

The question was not just his. It was a question for policy-makers, educators, business leaders- anyone who had the power to bridge the gap between education and employment. It was a question that demanded action.

As I looked out over the valley, watching the golden fields sway in the wind, the answer seemed both simple and complex: it wasn't about uprooting the youth from their homes, nor was it about forcing urban solutions onto rural landscapes. It was about giving them the tools to create, to innovate, to build something that belonged to them.

And as we continued down that quiet, sunlit path, his question no longer felt like a plea but a call to action. It was as if he were asking the world, "Are you willing to invest in us, to see our potential not only as labor for the cities but as the lifeblood of our communities?"

When we finally reached the village, I could still feel the weight of his words, and I knew I would carry them long after our conversation ended. Because his question, simple and profound, had left me with one of my own: **What if we** could turn the education that once promised a way out into the very force that lets them stay and thrive?

Weight of crimson and gold

The air in Mehandipur Balaji shimmered with the golden hues of late afternoon, the sun dipping lazily beyond the horizon. The scent of incense curled through the narrow streets, mingling with the distant clang of temple bells. This was a place of faith, of miracles whispered and prayers uttered in hushed reverence. But beneath the fervour of devotion, a different reality lingered, heavy and unspoken.

She sat on a low stone wall, beneath the gnarled limbs of a weary tree, its shade offering little solace against the weight of her fate. The crimson sari clung to her frail frame, embroidered with gold thread that gleamed defiantly in the waning sunlight. A cascade of glass bangles adorned her delicate wrists, their soft jingling a cruel mockery of celebration. In her arms, a baby stirred, a whimper escaping its tiny lips before settling back into uneasy sleep.

I approached her, a stranger in this village, drawn to the solemnity in her eyes. There was no fear, no hope, only a weary curiosity.

"Is he yours?" I asked gently, my eyes flickering between her and the infant.

For a moment, she hesitated, then nodded. The movement was barely perceptible, her expression unreadable.

I crouched beside her, searching for words that might bridge the chasm between us. "What is his name?"

She looked down at the sleeping child. "Arun," she murmured.

It was a name that meant 'sunrise,' yet her world had only known dusk.

Child marriage is not a union; it is a surrender. A girl, not yet a woman, handed over before she understands the depth of the vows she is expected to honor. In villages like this one, the practice is ingrained, justified by tradition and economic necessity. A daughter married young is one less mouth to feed, one less burden to carry.

Her husband was twice her age, her inlaws strangers who quickly became masters. They dictated when she woke, when she slept, what she ate, what she wore. Even the body she inhabited was no longer hers to command. Each night, she braced herself for his touch, the weight of obligation pressing down as heavily as the gold embroidery on her sari.

I shifted, brushing dust from my hands. "Did you want this?" I questioned.

Her lips parted, then pressed shut. Want. The word did not belong to her.

The cries of a baby cut through the evening air, a reminder that the weight she bore extended beyond her own suffering. Motherhood had come not as a choice, but as inevitability. Her body, too young to carry life, had nearly failed her. The memory of the pain still haunted her, a shadow that followed her every step.

"I used to go to school," she offered, surprising herself with the confession. "I liked numbers."

I smiled. "You were good at math?"

She nodded. "The teacher said I was the best in class." A pause. "But I stopped going after- " She gestured vaguely to the baby, to the vermillion in her parted hair, to the invisible shackles that held her here.

Education is the first casualty of child marriage. A girl who once solved equations is now expected to solve the riddles of survival- how to endure, how to please, how to navigate a world that does not belong to her. Her schoolbooks were traded for recipes, her pencils for sewing needles, her dreams for a life prescribed by others.

I exhaled slowly. "If you could go back, would you?"

A bitter smile played at the corners of her lips. "They won't let me."

The temple bells rang, their resonance a call to faith. Yet faith had not saved her. The gods had not intervened when she was led away in a bridal palanquin, the songs of celebration drowning out her silent pleas.

"Do you have friends here?" I asked.

She shook her head. Marriage had severed those ties, isolating her in a household where she was expected to serve, not belong. The walls of her new home were not just physical; they were barriers between her and the world she once knew.

Isolation is a wound that festers. Cut off from support, these girls become shadows, their suffering unseen, their voices unheard. Anxiety settles in their bones, depression seeps into their thoughts. Some endure. Others do not.

I saw the unspoken words in her eyes. "You deserve more than this."

A flicker of something, maybe anger crossed her face. "Deserve?" she echoed. "What does that matter?"

The streets of Mehandipur Balaji pulsed with life. Devotees came seeking blessings, their prayers carried on the wind. Yet, how many prayed for girls like her? How many saw her, truly saw her?

Change, when it comes, is slow. Laws exist, but enforcement falters. Communities cling to old ways, believing marriage protects girls when, in reality, it cages them. The path forward is paved with education, with empowerment, with voices that refuse to be silenced.

I rose, brushing off dust. "What if someone could help you? What if you could study again?"

She looked down at Arun, tracing a finger along his tiny cheek. "It's too late."

It was not too late. But she did not believe that yet.

I offered a final smile. "Maybe one day, you'll find a way."

She said nothing. But as I walked away, she held Arun a little closer, her grip a little stronger.

And somewhere, deep within, a spark remained.

As I left Mehandipur Balaji, the image of that girl lingered in my mind, her silent story echoing within me. The vibrant colors of the village faded into the background, replaced by the stark reality of her situation. Each step away from the village felt heavier, weighed down by the burden of what I had witnessed. I couldn't shake the feeling that her life, with all its unfulfilled potential, was emblematic of a larger crisis, one that affected countless young girls across the region and beyond.

What struck me most was the contrast between the celebrations around me and the girl's muted existence. While the bells rang joyfully and incense filled the air, her reality was defined by responsibility and expectation. I began to ponder the societal norms that upheld such practices. How could traditions, once rooted in community and culture, become shackles that bind the very youth they are meant to cherish?

The question that weighed heavily on my heart was: **What can we, as a society, do to break the chains of child marriage and empower young girls like her to reclaim their futures?** This was not just a question of individual stories, but a call to action for communities and nations.

Education emerged as a critical piece of the puzzle. Access to quality education can illuminate paths previously obscured by ignorance and tradition. By equipping girls with knowledge and skills, we can enable them to envision futures that extend beyond early marriage and domesticity. Schools can serve as safe havens, nurturing their aspirations and giving them the tools to advocate for their rights.

Moreover, community engagement is essential. Change cannot come solely from external influences; it must resonate from within. Conversations that challenge outdated norms and celebrate the value of girls' education and autonomy can shift perceptions. Empowering local leaders, parents, and elders to understand the importance of delaying marriage can foster an environment that supports girls' dreams rather than stifling them.

Legal frameworks also play a crucial role. Stronger laws against child marriage, coupled with robust enforcement, can protect vulnerable girls. However, legislation alone is not enough. It must be accompanied by grassroots campaigns that raise awareness and empower communities to uphold these laws, making them more than just words on paper.

Additionally, providing support systems for girls who resist early marriage is vital. Access to counseling, mentorship programs, and safe spaces can encourage them to pursue their goals, even in the face of societal pressure. When girls see role models who have successfully navigated similar challenges, it ignites hope and inspires change.

As I continued my journey away from Mehandipur Balaji, the image of that girl remained etched in my mind- a poignant reminder of the challenges still faced by so many. The call to action felt urgent and necessary. The question now loomed larger than ever: **How can we mobilize our**

collective efforts to ensure that no girl is forced to abandon her dreams?

It is a responsibility we all share, to cultivate a world where young girls can dream freely, pursue education, and choose their paths. By **working together-** communities, governments, and individuals- we can strive to break the chains of child marriage, empowering girls to reclaim their futures and rewrite their stories, filled with hope and possibility.

Waiting to be treated... If ever

The heavy white walls of AIIMS Delhi loomed over the hospital corridors like silent witnesses to countless untold stories. The smell of antiseptic hung thick in the air, mingling with the hushed murmurs of anxious families and the occasional urgent clatter of a stretcher wheeled past. Here, within these walls, life and death coexisted, separated only by the narrow margins of medical intervention and fate.

I had come to visit an acquaintance, but as I navigated the labyrinth of hallways, I found myself drawn to a different encounter. A middle-aged man sat hunched on a bench outside a consulting room, his hands clasped together in a silent act of endurance. His face, etched with deep lines, told a story of hardship, of miles traveled and hopes tempered by reality.

I sat down beside him, offering a small nod. "My name's Hemant," I said, extending my hand.

The man took it with a firm grip. "Anantram," he replied. His voice was steady but carried an undercurrent of exhaustion. "From Chhattisgarh. A small village." He paused, as if those few words were enough to paint a picture of his world. A place where life revolved around the seasons, where resilience was not a choice but a necessity.

After a moment's silence, I asked, "What brings you here?"

Anantram exhaled slowly. "My son. He's got something serious. The doctor here says it's an infection."

There was a weight in those words, an unspoken history of struggle. I leaned forward. "How long has he been sick?"

Anantram hesitated. "Since he was a boy. Maybe eight or nine years." His voice was barely above a whisper. "He's eighteen now."

A silence stretched between us, heavy with the implications of what had just been said. I struggled to comprehend the idea of a child going untreated for nearly a decade.

"Didn't you try to get him treated earlier?"

Anantram gave a rueful smile, his eyes clouded with something between regret and resignation. "We did. With what we had. We took him to the local healer. He gave him herbs and powders. But the cough didn't leave. It just got worse over time."

In many villages across India, traditional medicine was not just an alternative, it was often the only option. With hospitals miles away and proper doctors scarce, people placed their faith in what was accessible. The consequences, however, were often dire.

"What about other illnesses? Fever? Wounds?" I asked, trying to grasp the extent of the issue.

"It's the same," Anantram said. "People fall sick, and they wait. Sometimes a fever goes away on its own, sometimes it doesn't. Sometimes a wound heals, sometimes it festers. It's all left to fate. We do what we can, but there are no guarantees."

His words painted a grim picture, one that contrasted starkly with the bustling hospital around us. Here, medical professionals rushed from room to room, patients received treatment within hours, and pharmacies stocked every conceivable remedy. But in Anantram's world, time was not a resource people could afford to waste on waiting for help that rarely came.

"Isn't the government doing anything?" I pressed.

Anantram let out a quiet sigh. "There's a small clinic in the nearest town, twenty kilometers away. It opens once a week. The doctor comes, prescribes medicines, and leaves. By the time we get there, it's often too late."

The contrast between urban and rural healthcare was stark. In places like Delhi, specialists were available at a moment's notice, while in villages like Anantram's, a doctor was a fleeting presence- a visitor rather than a constant.

"And health camps? Aren't there programs to help?"

"They come. Sometimes. A few times a year, maybe. They set up for a day, see as many people as they can, and then they're gone." Anantram looked down at his hands. "We've learned to manage. To survive. But it's hard."

I felt a deep sense of sorrow and quiet anger. It wasn't just a lack of doctors but it was a lack of infrastructure, of priority. Healthcare was not a privilege, yet for millions, it remained just that. How had it come to this? How could a country progressing so rapidly leave entire communities behind?

I thought about the implications. How many children had died from fevers that could have been cured with a few pills? How many mothers had lost their lives in childbirth for want of basic prenatal care? How many stories like Anantram's remained unheard, buried beneath statistics and policy debates?

Anantram's face bore the weight of silent patience, a lifetime of waiting for change that never came. "What will happen when I go back to my village?" he asked, his voice quiet but unwavering. "Will things ever change?"

The question lingered in the air, an unspoken challenge to a system that had failed him and countless others. There were no easy answers. No quick fixes. But one thing was clear- this was not just about access to medicine. It was about justice. About equity. About the fundamental right to health.

The hospital corridor remained busy, its rhythm uninterrupted by the quiet conversation taking place within it. But for me, the world outside AIIMS had shifted. It was no longer just about the privilege of treatment- it was about those who had none at all.

As Anantram looked at me, the depth of his silent struggle evident in his eyes, I knew this story would stay with me. The problem was not just a policy failure; it was a moral failure. And unless something changed, unless people cared enough to make a difference, the question would continue to echo in the silence of villages across the country

How could we bring healthcare to every corner, to every Anantram who waits patiently, hoping against hope that someday, someone will care enough to make a difference? This was not merely a logistical issue of establishing clinics or sending healthcare workers into rural areas. It was a matter of awareness, of accessibility, and of fundamentally changing the narrative around healthcare in our country.

All these thoughts circled back to one fundamental question: How can we ensure that everyone, regardless of where they live, has access to the healthcare they deserve? It is a question that transcends policy and technology, reaching into the very heart of our societal values. Are we, as a nation, willing to prioritize health equity? Are we ready to confront the discomfort that comes with acknowledging these disparities?

As I sat in that bustling hospital, the voices of patients and doctors swirling around me, I realized that change requires more than just awareness- it demands action, It demands advocacy. It calls for each of us to become stewards of health equity, to raise our voices in support of those like Anantram and his son who should never have to wait in silence for care that is their right.

The challenge felt monumental, yet the hope flickered like a flame- a testament to the potential for change when awareness meets action. We can't afford to let that flame extinguish. It is in the quiet, persistent hope of individuals like Anantram that we find our purpose: to champion a future where no one waits in vain for the care they need.

In the end, the question remains: **How can we, as a society, transform that hope into a reality, ensuring that every Anantram has access to the healthcare they need and deserve?**

Scraps of survival

The sky over Delhi was a dull, smog streaked grey as the city hummed with its usual chaos. Samaypur Badli Metro Station bustled with people-officegoers hurrying to work, students slinging backpacks over their shoulders, and vendors shouting out their morning wares. Amid the rhythm of footsteps and the metallic chime of train doors sliding open and shut, I noticed a boy sitting outside the station entrance, his sharp eyes scanning the crowd. He was small for his age, dressed in a threadbare shirt that had once been white, his feet bare against the concrete floor. His name was Munna.

At ten years old, Munna had already learned how to navigate the invisible corridors of survival that the city's poor tread daily. He knew where to find discarded plastic bottles worth a few rupees, which corners of the market were more likely to have leftovers tossed aside, and how to disappear when the municipal officers came through, shooing away those like him as if they were an infestation rather than children.

As I waited for my friend, shifting my weight from foot to foot, Munna caught my attention. He seemed curious, observant.

"Are you waiting for someone?" Munna asked, his voice light, as if the question were merely out of curiosity rather than a strategic approach.

I looked down, surprised at first, then softened. "Yeah, a friend. What about you?"

"My mother is working nearby," Munna answered. "Sometimes I help her with ragpicking."

I saw the flicker of recognition cross my face- ragpickers, the people who sift through the city's refuse, the ones who existed in the background, unseen yet indispensable.

"Ragpicking must be challenging work," I said, crouching slightly to meet Munna's gaze. "What do you usually collect?"

"Plastic, metal, anything people throw away," Munna replied, his fingers tracing patterns on the dusty ground. "But it's not just that. It's dangerous too. We sift through a lot of garbage, and there are sharp things, dirty things- sometimes even chemicals. You never know what you might touch."

Many people never thought about the hidden dangers lurking in waste. Discarded glass shards, rusting metals, and hospital waste mixed with household trash, turning a livelihood into a gamble with health. The stench of decay and the swarming flies were the least of their problems.

"That sounds really tough," I admitted. "Do you wear any protective gear?"

Munna let out a laugh, a mixture of bitterness and disbelief. "Protective gear? We can't afford that. We just have to be careful. But sometimes, no matter how careful you are, you get hurt. There's no healthcare for us either, so a small cut can become a big problem."

A minor infection could fester, turning deadly in the absence of antibiotics. There were no safety nets for people like Munna and his mother, no insurance, no paid sick days. A single illness could mean the difference between eating for the week or going hungry.

"What about school?" I asked gently. "Do you get a chance to go?"

Munna looked away, his fingers stilling on the ground. "I wish. But my mother needs my help, and we can't lose the little money we make. It's hard enough as it is. If I went to school, who would help her?"

Education was a luxury when survival was uncertain. Even those who dreamed of school often found themselves tethered to necessity, their childhoods traded for work that society barely acknowledged.

"That must feel really limiting," I murmured. "What do you dream about?"

Munna hesitated, then, as if confessing a secret, whispered, "I want to be a teacher. I want to help other kids who can't go to school. But every day, it feels more impossible. If I could just get an education..."

Hope was dangerous when the odds were stacked so high. It flickered like a candle in the wind, easily snuffed out by hunger, sickness, or the unyielding demands of survival.

I exhaled, struggling to reconcile the bright eyed boy in front of me with the bleak future that seemed almost inevitable.

"It's not fair that you're trapped like this, doing work that most people don't even think about. Your efforts are so important, yet society doesn't see you."

Munna straightened, his voice firm. "Exactly. People don't understand that we're helping them. They just see us as dirty, as less than. But we're part of this city. Without us, the streets would be worse."

Cities relied on people like Munna- silent, unseen laborers who kept the wheels turning, yet remained outside the system that benefited from their work. Without formal recognition, they were disposable, their contributions unnoticed, their struggles ignored.

"And what about where you live? Is it safe?"

A shadow passed over Munna's face. "We live near the dump. It's crowded and dirty. When it rains, everything floods. There's no clean water, and we get sick often. Sometimes I just want a clean place to sleep."

The slums were temporary in the eyes of the government, but permanent for those who lived there. Evictions loomed like storms, unpredictable and devastating. Even the most fragile sense of stability could be ripped away overnight.

"How do you cope with all of that?" I asked, genuinely wanting to understand.

Munna shrugged. "We just keep going. It's all we can do. But sometimes it feels like we're running in circles. We need help, but nobody really listens to us."

"Maybe more people should hear your story," I suggested. "Awareness can spark change. If more people understood the challenges you face, they might be inspired to help."

Munna's eyes lit up for a moment, then dimmed again. "That's what I hope. But it's hard to believe anyone would care. We're just invisible to them."

But invisibility was an illusion, a convenient way for society to turn its gaze elsewhere. The reality was stark- without intervention, without acknowledgment, the cycle would persist, binding generation after generation in the same struggle.

As the train approached, I felt a rush of emotions. I had come here for a simple meeting, yet I was leaving with a weight on my heart. "You're not invisible, Munna. Your voice matters, and sharing it is a step toward change. If we could find ways to support people like you, through education, healthcare, and recognition of your work, maybe the future could be different."

Munna looked up, a flicker of determination crossing his face. "I want that. I want to show people that we're more than what they think we are."

The boy outside the station remained where he was, watching the city move around him. He had learned long ago that life did not pause for those left behind. But for the first time in a long while, he allowed himself a small thought: Maybe, just maybe, someone had truly heard him today.

As I prepared to board the train, I felt the weight of our conversation settle around me. Munna's struggles were a stark reminder of the realities faced by many living on society's margins. I stepped onto the train, pondering one question: **How can we, as a community, ensure that every voice is heard and every life is valued, especially for those fighting to break the cycle of poverty?**

Embers of division

The heat of the afternoon hung heavy over Bahraich, the air thick with dust and tension. The scent of smoldering ash lingered in the streets, a stark reminder of the chaos that had erupted only days ago. Broken glass crunched underfoot as Meera navigated her way through the remnants of what was once a thriving marketplace. Shops lay in ruins, their doors shattered, their shelves looted. The echoes of violence still resonated in the eerie silence.

Her phone was a lifeline in that moment- a tether to a world beyond the madness. As she dialled my number, she felt the weight of the past few days press against her chest.

"Hello? Is this a good time?" she asked, her voice trembling.

"Of course, Meera. What's going on?" I replied, sensing the urgency.

Meera swallowed hard. "It's... it's been a rough few days here. There was a small incident that escalated into something terrible. A disagreement, just a small one, but it turned into communal riots between Hindus and Muslims."

She knew how absurd it sounded- how a seemingly trivial misunderstanding could unravel into destruction. But that was the nature of fear, of unchecked fury. It did not ask questions; it did not listen to reason. It consumed.

"What happened exactly?" I asked, bracing myself.

She exhaled sharply, the images flashing before her eyes. "It started over something trivial, a misunderstanding about a festival or a gathering. But then uneducated people, people who don't really understand the broader implications, took it as a reason to lash out. They believed it was a matter of religion, and suddenly, everything turned violent."

Silence stretched between us, the kind that carried the weight of comprehension.

"Violent? What did they do?" I asked, my heart racing at the thought of destruction.

"They attacked local shops, set fire to properties, and it spiraled out of control," she said, her voice strained. "I couldn't believe my eyes when I saw people I knew- neighbors turning on each other over something so senseless. It was like a wave of madness washed over them."

In the span of mere hours, the town had transformed into a battlefield. Homes were no longer homes; they were sites of siege. The divide that once felt invisible had been drawn in blood and flames. This was not just about religion- it never was. It was about anger, desperation, and a deeply ingrained history of division, one that had been stoked and exploited time and again.

"That's devastating. Did anyone get hurt?" I asked.

"Yes, several people were injured. The police had to step in, but by then, it was chaos. All of this happened because of unverified rumors and misinformation spread on social media. It's like these people forgot their humanity."

Meera's voice wavered. The tragedy lay not just in the destruction but in how easily it had been provoked. One whisper, one false message forwarded without thought, and the embers had caught flame.

"It's alarming how easily fear and ignorance can ignite violence. But why do you think they reacted this way?" I pressed.

She sighed, her gaze drifting over the charred remains of a once-busy tea stall. "It's a mix of factors. Many people here are uneducated, struggling to make ends meet. When they hear something that stokes their fears, something that seems to threaten their way of life, they react without thinking. They don't stop to question if what they're hearing is true."

Fear is a powerful tool. It is a weapon wielded by those who seek control, those who thrive in chaos. It blinds people to reason and binds them to destruction. Generations had lived under the shadow of communal tension, and each new conflict only deepened the fault lines.

"That's a troubling cycle," I murmured. "So many lives can be ruined over misunderstandings and a lack of critical thinking."

"Exactly! And once the violence starts, it's hard to stop. People get caught up in the mob mentality. Friends turn against friends. Neighbors become enemies. All it takes is one spark, and it consumes everything."

I thought of the Patel brothers, who had lived beside the Ahmeds for decades, sharing meals, celebrating festivals together. Now, they refused to meet each other's eyes, the gulf between them widened by a single night of madness. How fragile was this harmony they had built? How easily had it been shattered?

"How do you think this could be prevented in the future?" I asked.

"There needs to be more education, not just about religion but about community and coexistence. People need to learn how to critically assess what they hear and not just take it at face value. We need to promote dialogue and understanding between communities, especially among the youth.”

“That sounds like a vital step. But how do we encourage that in a place where tensions run high?”

Meera paused, her mind racing through the possibilities. “It starts small. Community leaders and educators can organize workshops, discussions that bring people together. We need to humanize each other again, to remember that we are all part of this community. Building empathy is essential.”

She knew the road ahead would be long. Healing would take time, perhaps even generations. But it had to start somewhere. The alternative was unthinkable- a future where fear dictated their lives, where children grew up learning to distrust rather than embrace.

“I agree,” I said, feeling a sense of hope in her words. “But it seems like a long road ahead.”

“Yes, it is,” she said, standing amidst the ruins of her town. “But we can’t give up. If we don’t start these conversations now, who will? We have to plant the seeds of understanding and let them grow."

As our conversation continued, the weight of the moment settled between us. This was not just about Bahraich. It was about every town, every city that had been scarred by communal violence. It was about history repeating itself in cycles of pain and vengeance. But it was also about the possibility of change, of breaking free from those cycles.

As I ended the call, Meera looked around at her hometown- broken, but not beyond repair. The path to peace was steep, but with collective effort and a commitment to nurturing compassion, perhaps they could transform their community into a place of unity, rather than a battleground of division.

And so, as the sun began its descent, she took a deep breath and stepped forward, ready to begin the difficult but necessary work of rebuilding- not just walls, but trust, understanding, and hope.

As we wrapped up our call, I felt the weight of her final question lingering in my mind: **How can we build a society where differences are celebrated instead of feared?** How can we ensure that the cycle of violence ends with us? It was a profound challenge, one that demanded introspection and action. The path to understanding and peace was steep, but with collective effort and a commitment to nurturing compassion, perhaps we could transform our communities into havens of unity, rather than battlegrounds of division

The Bridge

The air in Kashi carried the weight of history, as if the past whispered through the narrow alleys and temple bells. The city breathed in the scent of marigolds and incense, its ghats echoing with the murmur of pilgrims and scholars alike. It was here, near Banaras Hindu University, that I found myself caught in an age-old debate- one that Ayush had lived through in more ways than one.

Ayush, my friend from college, had come from a small village in Bihar. His journey to academia had not been paved with ease; it had been a road of struggle, of proving himself at every step. That evening, as we sat at a roadside tea stall, listening to a group of students argue about India's reservation policies, I realized how deeply personal this conversation was for him.

A bespectacled student, his face alight with conviction, gestured animatedly. "The policy is necessary, no doubt about it. But should someone who went to a prestigious private school get the same quota as a kid from a rural, underfunded government school? How is that fair?"

Another student, his backpack worn from use, nodded. "Exactly! Reservation should be for those who actually need it. Not for those who already have financial stability."

I noticed Ayush tracing the rim of his cup, lost in thought. I knew what was going through his mind- his father, a farmer struggling against an unforgiving land, his mother stitching clothes late into the night to ensure he had books for school. The policy had been his bridge, the very reason he had managed to reach where he was today. But he had seen, too, how the system had gaps, how some benefited more than others.

I nudged him. "What do you think, Ayush?"

He took a measured breath before speaking. "I think reservation is like a bridge. Some of us need it to cross a river, but others might only need a small step. The problem is, the system doesn't differentiate between the two."

The students turned to him, intrigued by his metaphor.

"So what's the solution?" one of them asked.

Ayush chose his words carefully. "A more refined system. One that takes economic background into account along with social disadvantage. Caste-based discrimination is real and still exists, but so does economic disparity. If we refine the policy to help the truly disadvantaged, it would be fairer."

His words lingered in the air, carried by the soft hum of the night. The issue was complex, layered with history, injustice, and the desperate need for reform.

Reservation policies in India have long been a double-edged sword. Designed as a means of rectifying historical wrongs, they have undeniably changed lives. But their application, broad and often blind to economic conditions, has sparked debates across generations. The notion of equality is not about treating everyone the same- it is about acknowledging that people start from vastly different points in life. A Dalit student from an impoverished village, with no access to quality education, faces an entirely different set of challenges than someone from the same category whose family has climbed the economic ladder.

The conversation continued as Ayush and I walked towards the ghats, the Ganges shimmering under the soft glow of floating diyas. The smell of incense mingled with the distant chants from temples, filling the night with a sense of quiet reverence.

I broke the silence. "Do you think people will ever stop needing reservation?"

Ayush exhaled, his gaze fixed on the river. "Not in our lifetime. Maybe not for generations. Because discrimination isn't just in laws- it's in mindsets, in systems, in everyday interactions. But that doesn't mean we shouldn't work to make the system better."

We stopped near the edge of the water, watching as a young boy, no older than ten, floated a diya on the river. His clothes were tattered, his feet bare, but his eyes shone with something pure- hope.

Ayush watched him and smiled. "Reservation is supposed to be for him. For those who wouldn't have a chance otherwise. If we can ensure that, then we're moving in the right direction."

I nodded. The temple bells echoed into the night, and as we turned back into the labyrinthine alleys of Kashi, I knew that the debate was far from over. But one thing was clear: the future of millions rested on getting it right.

Because the true measure of progress isn't in policies alone. It's in the hands that rise from the ground, reaching, grasping, and finally, crossing the bridge to a better life.

As we think about the future of reservation and its role in shaping our society, we are left with a question: **How can we refine our approach to ensure that reservation benefits those truly in need, without perpetuating dependence or overlooking others facing similar hardships?**

Preface to next volume

When I first set out to write Rural Realities, my goal was to share the voices and stories of the people I encountered in the villages of North India. By shedding light on issues like poverty, caste discrimination, environmental degradation, and resource strain, I hoped to bridge the divide between awareness and empathy. But as I was writing this book, I had a plethora of ideas to tackle these issues.

In this next edition, I aim to bring together insights and solutions from around the world, examining approaches that have succeeded in similar contexts. Through research, conversations with global experts, and analysis of impactful initiatives, I will share strategies that could potentially address these pressing rural challenges. From innovative agricultural practices and grassroots educational programs to sustainable economic models, this edition will explore what can be done to empower these communities and strengthen our collective future.

Thank you to everyone who has accompanied me on this journey. I am grateful for your support and encouragement, and I look forward to seeing where this collective effort can lead us.

Copyright

All rights reserved. No part of this book may be reproduced, stored in a retrieval system, or transmitted in any form or by any means- electronic, mechanical, photocopying, recording, or otherwise- without prior written permission from the author.

This book is a work of non-fiction. The events, places, and conversations are based on real experiences, interviews, and research. However, some names and identifying details may have been changed to protect the privacy of individuals.

www.ingramcontent.com/pod-product-compliance
Lightning Source LLC
Chambersburg PA
CBHW020503160726
47991CB00007B/2784